urban|i|city

DAVE ALLEN
DEL BARRETT
FRED BARRINGTON
NATASHA BENNETT
MIKE CHOPRA-GANT
ILYA FISHER
BRITTA GIERSCHE
JOHN KELLY

ROGER KELLY
GRAHAM LAND
SUSI LUARD
WENDY NOWAK
STEPHEN REED
ROMNEY TANSEY
JONATHAN TAYLOR
ROGER TOWELL

The Royal Photographic Society

The Royal Photographic Society
URBANICITY

Published by The Royal Photographic Society
Fenton House
122 Wells Road
Bath BA2 3AH
England
www.rps.org

Thanks to:
Nikon School
63-64 Margaret Street, London W1W 8SW

Editor:
Del Barrett
del@delbarrett.com

Book design & cover image:
Jonathan Taylor
jetacity@gmail.com

Printing and binding by:
Ripe Digital
Unit 1, Park Lane Industrial Estate
Corsham, Wiltshire SN13 9LG

Urbanicity

From dogs to windows, sixteen photographers explore themes of urbanicity.

London, Urban is a micro-group of the Royal Photographic Society's London Region.

Each member works on an individual project, documenting London through an urban lens: life, landmarks and landscapes; markets, moments and monuments; structures, steel and stone, the ordinary and the extraordinary of this ever evolving metropolis.

Urbanicity contains 16 unique visual stories.

Dave Allen LRPS
Lone Individuals in Urban London

London has one of the most fascinating urban environments in the world with amazing architecture, structures, open and enclosed spaces. The city has a resident population of about 8.5 million people and on average 15 million tourists visit London each year, not to mention the vast numbers of people commuting every day into the City to work.

Yet individual figures can be seen in London, contrasted by the City's built environment. They appear to be vulnerable, fragile, lost or even lonely.

My images attempt to capture these lone individuals in urban London.

Del Barrett ARPS
Mixed Doubles

A series of London-based photographs, where each
pair of images shares a common feature. Some are
obvious, some are not. Some are visible, some are
implied. Some are ordinary, some are bizarre. But
all are part of our rich urban fabric.

Fred Barrington ARPS
Windows - A Glimpse

I have always been fascinated by people's lives, although not necessarily by the people themselves.

They say the eyes are the window to the soul, but I prefer to concentrate on the windows.

Whilst people do not normally put things in their window for the gratification of outsiders, the contents from the outside can offer a possible glimpse into their lives, and with some imagination stories can be constructed, which are probably inaccurate.

The windows themselves are unimportant, they are simply the frames.

Natasha Bennett
London Vintage

I set out to capture the different aspects of the vibrant vintage scene in London. Despite the high tech world we live in, or may be because of it, vintage is flourishing.

The streets of Shoreditch are filled with vintage shops. Vintage frees us to inhabit other eras. This may be through wearing clothes or revelling in a vintage experience. I returned to one of my favourite haunts, Maison Bertaux, which is original, quirky and serves the finest patisserie in London. It may have a French name, but its eccentricity is very English. I also discovered new haunts, such as the Regency Cafe, a fantastic "greasy spoon", with amazing authentic 1940's interiors.

London also has its share of vintage travel, harking back to the style of a bygone age. Classic cars are to be found on London streets, in front of rows of Regency, Edwardian and Victorian townhouses. Their drivers yearn for spirited travel. At Victoria, the steam hauled Pullman still pulls out of the station, in a haze of white smoke, evoking the romance of the Victorian Age of Steam.

Vintage may be of the past, but it's still alive, bringing fun and romance to Londoners.

Mike Chopra-Gant ARPS
Estates of Utopia

Contemporary, pessimistic views of social housing - conditioned by decades of neoliberal marketization, and neglect of the social - are at odds with original idealism that underpinned the development of early-postwar social housing in London. These utopian ideals gave rise to buildings with higher aesthetic aspirations than are evident in more commonplace, purely functionalist, utilitarian designs that came to typify later mass housing projects. These images form part of a larger set exploring the residual traces of the utopian spirit still to be found in London's social housing.

Ilya Fisher
Urban Art

Many people roam London streets armed with their cameras, on the hunt for some great graffiti. However, my images aim to give examples of another kind of street art, just as fabulous but in a different way. It is out there, on London streets, waiting for us to notice and frame it. It's this bit of peeling paint or shredded poster, it's that rusty pipe or mouldy wall. It's the details we often walk past without noticing, framed into Urban Art.

Britta Giersche
Ricky's Garage | Leven Road London E14

I am interested in interior places. I like how the space and the objects contained within it bear witness to the people who occupy them and allow for an interpretation of historical, social or psychological behaviour. My photographs are one of many possible stories that could emerge from the spaces I document.

The photos for 'Ricky's Garage' were all taken on 4th March 2015 within a short space of time.

I met Ricky whilst looking for an industrial quayside warehouse on Leven Road in East London. He told me that it had recently been demolished to make room for a residential development – the building site was just opposite his garage.

The docklands in E14 were named one of the London property hotspots in 2015, promising investors a return of up to 35% in two years. Along with the building boom comes a picture boom in the form of advertising hoardings showing tall new structures and bright clean interiors.

Amongst many other things the photographs of Ricky's garage can be read as counterimages to the shiny display across the road.

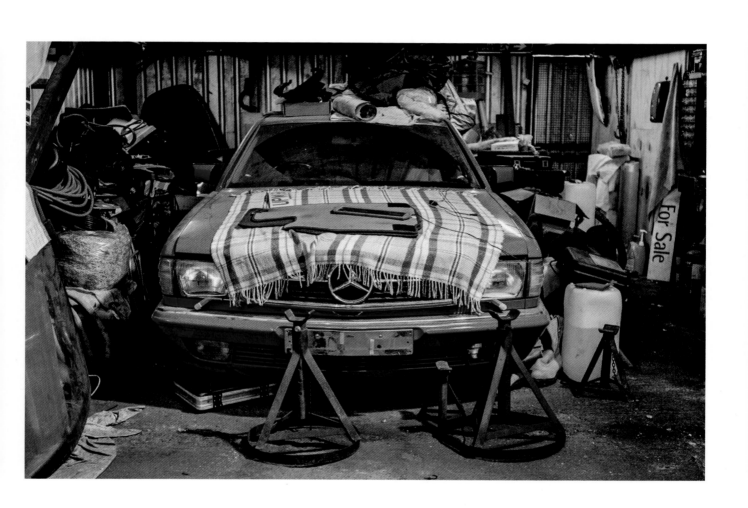

John Kelly LRPS
London As I Saw Her

As an adopted Londoner, originally from New Zealand, I wanted to record cultural iconic landmarks which have particularly caught my eye: St Paul's Dome designed by Sir Christopher Wren, dominating London's skyline since 1696. Albert Bridge (1870) and Tower Bridge (1886), both of strategic and economic importance. The ancient Tower of London (1078), here with the symbolic ceramic poppies marking the centenary of the outbreak of the First World War. The traditional British telephone box, introduced to London streets in 1926. London Transport's double decker Routemaster, introduced in 1956, and the Clock Tower keeping Londoners on time since 1859.

For me, this sequence of images captures the historic essence of urban London.

15 St Paul's Cathedral
Fleet Street
Aldwych

TOWER HILL

Royal Beasts

Royal Beasts

15

ALM 60B

Roger Kelly
Old Father

Some months ago the contributors to this book met in a small back room of a west end London pub and discussed individual projects for later publication.

As it worked out, I was one of the last to speak during the 'round robin' discussion and, to my amazement, no one had mentioned London's artery, Old Father Thames itself.

Being a regular visitor to the capital I often time my visits to match the low tide for some photography. Various mobile device applications assist with appropriate tide times, sun directions and good Thames shoreline access points.

It is often pot luck to discover what the receding water reveals and the following are documentary images illustrating some of the many scenes I have observed during my ambles along both banks.

Graham Land
London Markets

I've tried to portray something of the diversity of everyday life that can be seen in a London Market. These local markets vary greatly, both in their nature and custom, they are all about people.

The London metropolis has a wealth of such places. Some date back to the early middle-ages, others to the 19th century when Greater London's population mushroomed from 1 to 5 million. With the growth of the local high street and modern shopping mall many, such as the London Egg Exchange where over a billion eggs a year were sold, are now gone. However, in recent times there has been a revival with new 'Farmers' and other weekend-only markets coming into being.

The photographs were taken at a variety of locations: Borough Market (Southwark), Broadway Market (Hackney), Camden Market, East Street Market (Camberwell), Portobello Road & Golborne Road Markets (Notting Hill) and Surrey Street Market (Croydon).

Susi Luard
London Dogs

I love walking the streets of London and I love dogs. It is not practical for me to have a dog right now so the next best thing is to photograph them in different postal districts of London, from east to west and north to south. Shown here are dogs from Islington, Pedley Street E1, Woodford Green, Canary Wharf, Woolwich, Maltby Street SE1, Hampstead Heath, Rotherhithe and Covent Garden.

I did not encounter feral dogs and I would like to think they are all safely ensconced in dog rescue 'homes'. I came across working dogs such as the explosive sniffers patrolling Canary Wharf, pets and guard dogs (often ineffective with more bark than bite). They were large and small, boisterous and calm, across a large variety of breeds. Currently the most popular breed in London seems to be the Staffordshire bull terrier. To me, they are all adorable.

Wendy Nowak
Rotherhithe Heritage

For centuries Rotherhithe was a major gateway to the Port of London, handling goods, particularly timber, from all over the world and providing employment for many Londoners.

It was an area consisting mainly of docks, wharves and historic riverside pubs. The majority of the dock workers did not live in Rotherhithe itself.

By the early 1980s the docks were closed and the area was earmarked for redevelopment. Many of the warehouses have now been turned into apartment blocks and many of the former docks have been filled in. Rotherhithe has seen much regeneration over the past couple of decades.

My photographic mission was to catalogue the results of this regeneration and record how the legacy of the docks, which many of us here believe should be preserved, has been integrated into the modern, and ever-changing, face of Rotherhithe.

Stephen Reed
A Hairy Subject

I've long been fascinated by shopfronts, and I've photographed dozens, if not hundreds, since moving to London in 2011.

I have a soft spot for launderettes, cafés and especially barber shops and hair salons. In addition to their often quirky and clever names, barber shops and salons often say so much about the neighbourhoods where they're found. They beautifully illustrate the diversity of the city and the hopes and ambitions of individual small business owners.

These particular photos were taken all across greater London in locations including Tottenham, Kilburn, Leytonstone, Walthamstow, Catford, New Cross and in the heart of The City itself.

Romney Tansley ARPS
On the Edge of Town

My subject is the ephemeral ever-changing world on the urban periphery. The preserve of retail parks, filling stations and in-between areas ripe for demolition/redevelopment, it is rich with photographic opportunity.

Man-made surfaces, textures, colours, structures, shapes and their shadows, jostle together with the scant remnants of nature to form the intricate designs of a surreal landscape of our creating.

Hoardings and signage, fencing, street furniture and barriers of varying kinds, constructed from man-made materials, all weather-beaten and mostly past their best, are the raw material of my project.

In my fascination with this world I want my photography to raise questions for the viewer about human consumption and consumerism - our throw-away society. But also to ask if it's possible for the camera to find beauty and harmony in the increasingly uniform and technological terrain of our lives.

All my images were taken on or close to the Purley Way in Croydon.

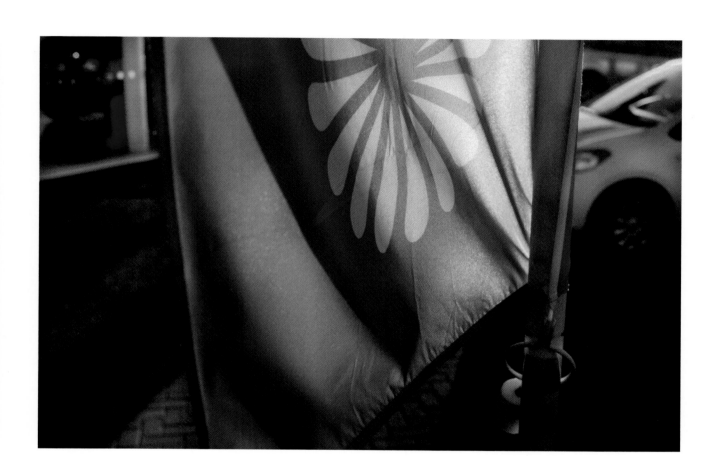

Jonathan Taylor
No Parking

In urban London, cars have proliferated as the population grows and more of us become owners. Roads are clogged in the diminishing spaces shared with buses, motorbikes and bicycles and the problem of where to park becomes more acute.

We don't care to walk so far to find a space which are now more limited by the councils' need for cash and the highway engineers' creation of safer highways. So the few garages and off-street parking spaces become more precious and so does our demand for clear access to these.

The preferred way to assert one's informal right to access seems to be the hand painted "No Parking" sign. Sometimes looking professional but more often not; they vary as much as the personalities producing them. Casual and homely or bold and ugly, well crafted and straight or running out of space, they have become a part of our streets.

Roger Towell ARPS
Great Eastern Street

My project shows some urban art. It is urban art rather than the more graffiti based "street art", particularly around the inner London city area of Shoreditch.

I focussed on one building in Great Eastern Street whose exterior is repainted vividly and colourfully, on a regular basis. I visited the street many times, each visit a few weeks apart and took the images from the same spot across the street. The changing face of the building emphasises the ephemeral nature of the artwork over time.

Given the subject matter, all the images are in colour – obviously the project just would not work in monochrome.

Photographers

Dave Allen	LRPS	
Del Barrett	ARPS	delbarrett.com
Fred Barrington	ARPS	
Natasha Bennett		
Mike Chopra-Gant	ARPS	radiantcity.photography
Ilya Fisher		ilyafisher.com
Britta Giersche		brittagiersche.wordpress.com
John Kelly	LRPS	flickr.com/photos/jomak1
Roger Kelly		
Graham Land		flickr.com/photos/photoviator
Susi Luard		flickr.com/photos/88588024@N03/
Wendy Nowak		
Stephen Reed		flickr.com/photos/sreed99342
Romney Tansley	ARPS	rps.org/member/profile/romney-tansley
Jonathan Taylor		jetfoto.co.uk
Roger Towell	ARPS	rogertowellphotography.com

LONDON, URBAN